First Facts

American Symbols

The White House

by Debbie L. Yanuck

Consultant:
Melodie Andrews, Ph.D.
Associate Professor of Early American History
Minnesota State University, Mankato

Capstone *press*

Capstone Press
151 Good Counsel Drive, P.O. Box 669, Mankato, Minnesota 56002
http://www.capstone-press.com

Library of Congress Cataloging-in-Publication Data
Yanuck, Debbie L.
  The White House / by Debbie L. Yanuck.
    p. cm.—(American symbols)
  Summary: A simple introduction to the White House, including its history, designer, construction, location, and importance as a symbol of the United States.
    Includes bibliographical references and index.
    ISBN 0-7368-1633-X (hardcover)
    1. White House (Washington, D.C.)—Juvenile literature. 2. White House (Washington, D.C.)—History—Juvenile literature. 3. Presidents—United States—History—Juvenile literature. 4. Washington (D.C.)—Buildings, structures, etc.—Juvenile literature. [1. White House (Washington, D.C.) 2. Presidents—History. 3. Washington (D.C.)—Buildings, structures, etc.] I. Title. II. American symbols (Mankato, Minn.)
F204.W5 Y36 2003
975.3—dc21   2002010710

Editorial Credits

Chris Harbo and Roberta Schmidt, editors; Eric Kudalis, product planning editor;
    Linda Clavel, cover and interior designer; Alta Schaffer, photo researcher

Photo Credits

Abbie Rowe, National Park Service, courtesy Harry S. Truman Library, 15
AP Photo/Wilfredo Lee, 5
Maryland Historical Society, Baltimore, Maryland, 11, 20
Painting by Gordon Phillips, White House Collection, White House Historical Association
    (127), 13
PhotoDisc, cover, 21
Photo Network/Patti McConville, 7
Photri-Microstock, 9, 14, 16, 17; Lani Novak Howe, 19

1 2 3 4 5 6 08 07 06 05 04 03

Table of Contents

White House Fast Facts

⭐ In 1792, Thomas Jefferson held a contest to find an architect for the White House.

⭐ John Adams was the first president to live in the White House.

⭐ The White House is located in Washington, D.C.

⭐ In 1814, the British army set fire to the White House. Only the outside walls survived the fire.

⭐ In 1901, President Theodore Roosevelt gave the White House its name. Before then, it was called the President's Palace or the Executive Mansion.

⭐ The White House has 132 rooms.

⭐ The White House is the only house of any world leader that regularly gives free tours.

American Symbol of Democracy

The White House is a symbol of
democracy. A democracy is a
government whose members are
elected by its people. Every four
years, Americans elect a president.
The White House is the president's
home and office.

elect
to choose someone by voting

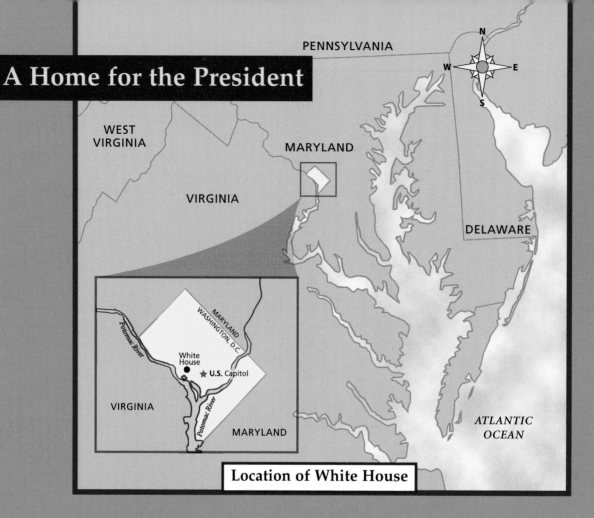

Location of White House

In 1789, George Washington became the first U.S. president. He lived in New York City and in Philadelphia. In 1790, Congress passed the Residence Act to build a new

capital city. Today, the city is called
Washington, D.C. The president's house
would be built near the Potomac River.

The Contest

In 1792, Thomas Jefferson held a contest to design the White House. Nine architects sent in drawings. A committee picked James Hoban's design. He was an Irish immigrant. Workers began to build the White House on October 13, 1792.

architect
a person who draws plans to show how buildings should look

President Adams Moves In

In 1800, John Adams moved into
the White House. He was the second
president of the United States. Only
six rooms were complete at that time.
John's wife Abigail used an unfinished
room to dry clothes. The house did not
have running water or a bathroom.

Changes to the White House

The White House has changed many times since 1800. During the War of 1812 (1812–1814), the British set fire to the White House. Workers rebuilt the inside.

In 1948, the inside of the White House was falling apart. Workers replaced many walls and floors. They made everything look the same as before.

The White House has 132 rooms. The State Dining Room seats more than 130 people. The White House library is filled with books by American authors.

The China Room has plates and cups from almost every presidency. The president and his family live on the second floor.

The White House Today

More than one million people visit the White House each year. Every Easter, children can play games on the White House lawn. Throughout the year, people can walk through some of the rooms in the house. They see that the White House is a symbol of democracy.

Timeline

1792—A contest is held to find an architect to design the president's house.

1800—John Adams is the first president to move into the White House.

1790—Congress passes the Residence Act to build a new capital city near the Potomac River.

1792—Workers begin to build the White House on October 13.

1901—President Theodore Roosevelt gives the White House its name.

1814—The British set fire to the White House.

1948—Workers begin to rebuild most of the rooms in the White House.

Hands On: Plan a House

In 1790, James Hoban designed the White House. He made many drawings of the outside and inside of the president's home. If you were going to build a house, how would you design it? Try this activity to find out.

What You Need

Ruler   Toothpicks
Pencil   Glue
White paper   Crayons

What You Do

1. Use a ruler and a pencil to draw a large rectangle on a piece of paper. The four sides of the rectangle are the four outside walls of your house.
2. On the inside of the rectangle, draw walls to create rooms. Draw a dining room, a kitchen, a bathroom, a living room, and some bedrooms in your house.
3. Glue the toothpicks down on all of your walls.
4. Color each room with crayons. The White House has a Green Room, a Blue Room, and a Red Room. What colors are your rooms?
5. Name your house. The White House was once called the President's Palace and the Executive Mansion.

Words to Know

architect (AR-ki-tekt)—a person who draws plans that show how buildings should look

committee (kuh-MIT-ee)—a group of people chosen to do a special task

Congress (KONG-griss)—the branch of the U.S. government that makes laws

democracy (di-MOK-ruh-see)—a government in which people choose their leaders by voting

design (di-ZINE)—to make a plan of something that could be built

immigrant (IM-uh-gruhnt)—a person who leaves one country to live in another country

residence (REZ-uh-duhnss)—a place where someone lives

symbol (SIM-buhl)—an object that stands for something else

Read More

Grace, Catherine O'Neill. *The White House: The Official History for Children.* New York: Scholastic, 2003.

Gray, Susan Heinrichs. *The White House.* Let's See. Minneapolis: Compass Point Books, 2002.

Internet Sites

Track down many sites about the White House.

Visit the FACT HOUND at
http://www.facthound.com

IT IS EASY! IT IS FUN!

1) Go to *http://www.facthound.com*
2) Type in: 073681633X
3) Click on "FETCH IT" and FACT HOUND will find several links hand-picked by our editors.

Relax and let our pal FACT HOUND do the research for you!

Index